In Agitation

Ian Davidson

NEWTON-LE-WILLOWS

Published in the United Kingdom in 2014
by The Knives Forks And Spoons Press,
122 Birley Street,
Newton-le-Willows,
Merseyside,
WA12 9UN.

ISBN 978-1-909443-43-3

Copyright © Ian Davidson, 2014.

The right of Ian Davidson to be identified as the author of this work has been asserted by him in accordance with the Copyrights, Designs and Patents Act of 1988. All rights reserved. No part of this publication may be reproduced, stored in a retrieval system, transmitted in any form or by any means, electronic, photocopying, recording or otherwise, without prior permission of the publisher.

The cover image is by © Lara Pearson

Table of Contents

Head over heels	5
Lighting up	6
Weather Report	7
Potential difference	10
In agitation	11
Dust	13
Rentboy	15
Pocket	16
Repeat	17

The California Poems

Moving On	21
Car Show	22
Car Show 2	23
Ants 2	24

In Agitation

Head over heels

The moon losing its star as it
drifts to the north I see lights
breaking their backs their beams.

I hear tyres turn to liquid
rubber trying to hold the
road and can't be sure what moves

around what. Crows do tumble
turns against the evening sky
as traffic roars moon turns first

phase. Objects blurred and out of
focus. The time things stay to-
gether, star and moon, or drift

apart. The motion of the
spheres, the other side when we
fall as if forever and

tumbling through the orbit of the
moon past stars travelling
in tumble turns, head over heels.

Ian Davidson

Lighting up

Objects separated by
light like a parasol sus-
pended over the sea hold-
ing itself up. Birds flock to-

gether the little air be-
tween like elastic or a
shock absorber that pulls and
pushes. Sheep bunch, moving as

one object with no patch of
dark between them and holding
each other up, swerving like
sheep and all together. In

empty northern skies making
light of material no
thing moves except the long gone
sun still setting, lighting up.

In Agitation

Weather Report

1.

In the space between wind and
tide Clare awakes, he offers her
a lit cigarette. It was
their home town and the dust from

trucks passing as she sat in
her shed, thinking her children home.
Her features like crossed threads as
if the tap and die slipped in

the curve of light coming
out of lane control. In this
heat he adjusts his tie, walks
across the surface, sun spots.

2.

Passage became package, and
Clare was made to measure and
part of the counter culture,
leant across the service hatch breathing.

Ian Davidson

Wandering the taxi ranks
in search of feeling she would
talk with intensity until
dawn sometimes. When Clare hears the

voices both sides of her brain
try to balance it out. Click to
see my patents. Click if you are a
venture capitalist. She

speaks out loud looks anxiously
around, scared of being over-
heard in the language regions
of a limitless landscape.

Click again to hear my au-
ditory hallucina-
tions, beliefs I hold with ex-
tra ordinary convic-

tion, as if they are real. Click
to experience my
disorganised thinking and
inappropriate ways of

behaving, eccentric dress.
Click to hear shouting, swearing,
muttering aloud. Click to
hear the voices from next door.

In Agitation

3.

The shed door bangs in the wind.
Children cycle slowly home.
The cigarette burns to the end.
Brain becomes blizzard, snow storm.

Ian Davidson

Potential difference

Then went down to potential
difference or the geese fly
south and angled to the main

road or actuality.
And then to the earth's core where
the cold became warmth and in

wet air shivering neither
here nor there but half asleep
before crawling towards an

entrance that is maybe a
this or that. And performing
my potential, tumble turns.

In agitation

In agitation the bees
stirred up behind the ivy.
Mountains attempting immo-
bility fall into the

sea. There is friction. The bees
shake the ivy, the breeze shakes
the ivy, dust is kicked up
on distant trails, driven in.

At the edge of the solid
wave the water becomes white
then wet. Pieces of spray. The
end of the movement, just be-

fore rest, free of the ocean.
The banks that matter makes or
care. A lump slowly swallowed.
In the pit of my stomach.

I am jostled. I turn my
head to the sun and feel the
skin tighten at the edge of
my eye. Voices are incom-

Ian Davidson

prehensible. The centre
talks back to the frayed edges
that travelling has unra-
velled. Two boys kicking up dust.

In the hot air dryer uneven
layers, pits, craters, appear.
Flurries become itches to
scratch at a heavy heart, slow

to turn. Distrustful, defens-
ive, it begins to melt its
ventricles to the sun. A
heart stolen from the outer

estate, like low hanging fruit.
For those with little it is
easy to make up false pro-
mises or threats of fat ze-

ros in the Republic of
Rousillon and its Oc neigh-
bours. The sea wears at the shore
and the wind at the stand of

pines. The sun removes skin, flake
by flake, splits hairs, while at the
edge of an eyelids flutter,
bells clang quarters in half time.

In Agitation

Dust
For Diane di Prima

Directing his gaze towards
the scrapped metal and the per-
ambulator wheels the first

thing is to cut off all her
hair the second is to wheel
something out against the four

frail walls it is a matter
of style, wide open spaces,
walls falling to dust, and dust

falling in a curtain a-
cross the doorways, there is
nothing in the way we like

it, nothing in the ways we
don't like it. In moving from
home to home she found things out

about herself the many a-
partments she would wake up in
the many walls too weak to

Ian Davidson

hold secrets the times she sold
herself to an experiment.
The flesh shows its feelings
in expelled air or skin tones.

In Agitation

Rentboy

The material is a
thin veil, like a barrage ball-
oon. Or the temporary
Olympian structures that

can easily be cut. I
cannot trust in my imag-
ination. I never thought
it would return. Community

gardens slow blown tum-
ble weed, volunteer pota-
toes. Making things look like some
thing else or they too are cut

like branches from a fruit tree
that stored root material
for a future that may never material-
ise. The fight is for the pack-

aging and not the packed. Her
-i-tage. Leisure. Memories.

Ian Davidson

Pocket

Polly sees the silver sea
and moon behind high cloud. In
her agitation things churn,

wanting out. On the water-
front by the bandstand people
pray to the moon. Like an iron

curtain between two worlds the
sea fills any shape its pour-
ed into, repeatedly

running at the soft waves and
beaten back by the foam fall-
ing apart. Energy returns

to where it came from. Ah sea,
ah moon that moves it, troubled
love in her distressed surface,

what colours can she carry
home to light her little world.
She lives in Polly Pocket,

the lid casting its shadow.
Mighty Max reads the polished
marks on the base while Polly

In Agitation

patiently dusts, tries on her
new clothes, endlessly gener-
ating language and looking

at the moon without expre-
ssion and waiting for the words
to strike or the next big wave.

Ian Davidson

Repeat

Turning only lifting up
and then I do that thing a-
gain but repeat still alive
the gestures of filling out
forms resume sleep as the dog
barks or the pigeons come home
to roost. And then I do that
thing again there is smoke in
the air repeat like a furr-
ow in the brow or a brain
waves back from a distant shore
or like a swallow of the
summer or a cuckoo I
do that thing again digging in-
to the reserves where melo-
dies are made as an aid to
memory. Or then I do
that thing again, breaths between
the motion of the heart beat
and its rest.

The California Poems
(for Michael Davidson)

In Agitation

Moving On

And then went past the violent
yellow fields, cattle high
on the hill where the border
crosses and opens out in-

to a big sky. Cars passing
at speed, lift, cactii moving
past planets, world on its ax-
is crippled by repeti-

tion and doing it over.
Held to account. And what turns
Around. Smooth as ice, swifter
than an arrow shot from the

end of the country. Venus,
drifting, a dark disc, power
lines leading off into no-
where, fields lightened by

lack of rain. The train follows
tracks into the heart of it.
Evidence little enough,
fading, decaying material.

Ian Davidson

Car Show

Light's quick breaks on the cars head-
ing south. Planes all over the
place, fanning out below cloud
cover and the bands of white

and blue light. Pelicans make
holes in the sky, only dumb
critics abstract from the ac-
tual heat and the sun shining

off the hot cars to the cold
steel that made them, how things might
have been transforming base me-
tal, crude oil, material.

In Agitation

Car Show

With the immobility
of icons at the kerb re-
flecting light into light, emp-
ty shells whose function is on-

ly nostalgia and the gradu-
ation presents, future and pasts.
The earth does go round the sun.
The sun burns away cloud. Days

extend slowly, dogs pull. The
surface workers in their sun-
day best and chromed to death as
if plating over the evi-

dence of internal combus-
tion, spitting smoke and oil cars
going nowhere. Bruno burnt
as a heretic. The sun

sinks over an horizon.
Wander as under the moon
things thin down, the road narrows,
becomes tracks, parallel lines.

Ian Davidson

Ants

I'll never get over see-
ing the words one after the
other like the waves come in
from the Pacific swell and

under the pier where it all
happens and you write it down
for later. And I shouldn't, or
thought about it all that much.